CAMBRIDGE RAINBOW READING

Patterns in nature

Written by Moeneba Slamang

CAMBRIDGE UNIVERSITY PRESS

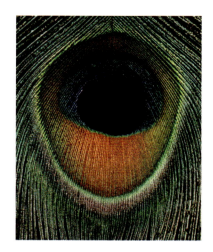

What is this that we see?
What do you think it could be?

Slices of bread spread around?
A porcupine turned upside down?

No, it's a pine cone from a pine tree.

What is this that we see?
What do you think it could be?

Old fish bones from last year?
The antlers of a green deer?

No, it's the pattern of veins on a leaf.

What is this that we see?
What do you think it could be?

A frightened owl's eye?
The mouth of a fly?

No, it's a feather of a peacock.

What is this that we see?
What do you think it could be?

Sleeping snakes lying in rows?
Sister's hair that grows and grows?

No, it's a sand dune.

What is this that we see?
What do you think it could be?

Tiles on a shop floor?
A decorated wooden door?

No, it's the shell of a tortoise.

What is this that we see?
What do you think it could be?

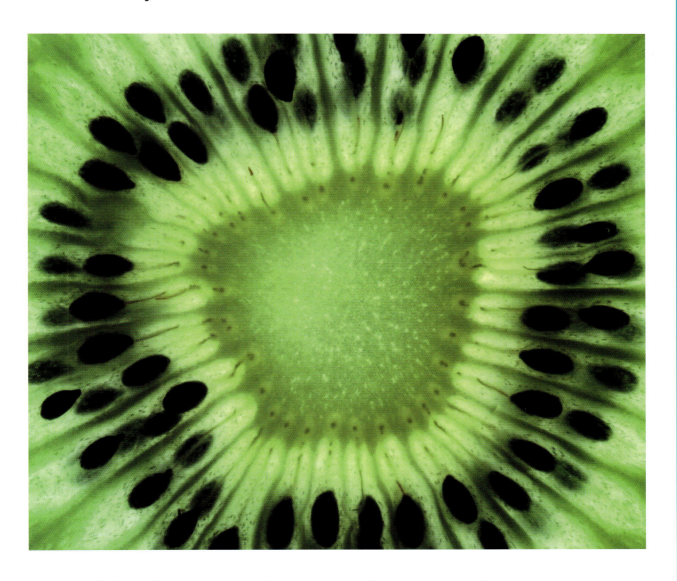

Little black bugs asleep in their nest?
The brooch Granny wears to look her best?

No, it's a kiwi fruit cut in half.

What is this that we see?
What do you think it could be?

Long, thin earthworms curled about?
A zebra's skin, without a doubt!

No, it's a fingerprint.
Could it belong to you?